Polar Bear
*Arctic Circle—Canada,
Greenland, Norway, Russia,
United States*

Orchid Mantis
Southeast Asia

Mimic Octopus
*Indo-Pacific Oceans—
New Caledonia,
Philippines,
Thailand, Indonesia,
Malaysia, Australia*

African Leopard
Sub-Saharan Africa

Ornate Wobbegong
*Pacific Ocean—
Eastern Australia*

Panther Chameleon
Madagascar

Leaf and Stick Insects
Australia

A NOTE FROM THE AUTHOR-ILLUSTRATOR

The animals hiding in these pages all have unique and impressive techniques for staying out of sight. Some change their colors and patterns to blend in with their surroundings, others disguise themselves as sticks or flowers, and one even wears a cloak of algae!

While they might all have different approaches to camouflage, each is dependent on a unique environment to make its camouflage work. From the savannas of Africa to the jungles of South America to the waters of the Pacific Ocean, these places are necessary for their survival.

At a time when their habitats are under threat because of climate change and other human activities, it's up to us to make sure we do all that we can to protect these incredible masters of disguise—even when we can't always see them!

First US edition 2021

Library of Congress Catalog Card Number 2021933917
ISBN 978-1-5362-1405-5

23 24 25 26 CCP 10 9 8 7 6 5 4 3 2

Printed in Shenzhen, Guangdong, China

This book was typeset in Gill Sans Medium.
The illustrations were done in watercolor, pencil, and digital collage.

Candlewick Studio
an imprint of
Candlewick Press
99 Dover Street
Somerville, Massachusetts 02144

www.candlewickstudio.com

MASTERS

OF

DISGUISE

Camouflaging Creatures & Magnificent Mimics

Marc Martin

CANDLEWICK STUDIO
an imprint of Candlewick Press

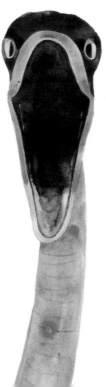

Panther Chameleon

Chameleons are known for their remarkable ability to change color to blend into their environment. These reptiles are often found in the treetops of tropical or mountain rain forests and grassland. Madagascar is home to almost half of the world's chameleon species, including the panther chameleon, one of fifty-nine chameleon species found nowhere else on the planet.

360-Degree View

Chameleons can rotate each eye nearly 180 degrees and focus each one independently, which means they can look at two things at once!

A Kaleidoscope of Colors

Like many chameleons, panther chameleons can change color with the help of special cells in their skin called chromatophores. These cells help the chameleon blend in with its environment and evade predators. It can also take on brighter colors to intimidate rivals or communicate with potential mates.

Sticky Situation

Not only is a chameleon's tongue about twice its body length, but a chameleon can shoot its tongue out of its mouth and hit its prey in about 0.007 seconds!

A Firm Grasp

Chameleons' five toes have evolved into groups. The forefoot has two outside toes joined together to form one group, and three inside toes form another; the hind foot has the opposite arrangement. This allows them to grasp branches and keep a grip while climbing.

Kaleidoscopic Camouflage

Have you heard of the helmet vanga, Schlegel's asity, red fody, comet moth, or tomato frog? They are just some of the unique creatures hiding in this forest, along with ten cleverly concealed chameleons!

Great Horned Owl

The great horned owl is the most common owl in the Americas, ranging from Alaska to Argentina. They live in many habitats, including forests, scrublands, marshes, deserts, and even urban areas.

Silent but Deadly

The owls' feathers are loosely packed and have soft saw-toothed edges that allow the birds to fly almost silently, making them stealthy hunters that can sneak up on their prey.

Grip

When clenched, the owls' strong talons require a force of 28 pounds (13 kilograms) to open. They use their grip to kill and carry prey several times heavier than themselves, such as falcons, ospreys, and raccoons.

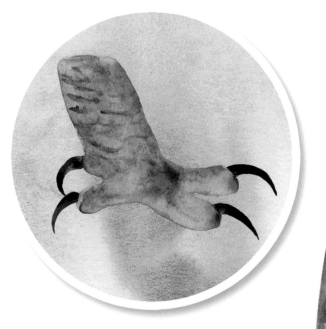

Eyes Everywhere

The great horned owls' large eyes have pupils that can open widely in the dark for excellent night vision. While their eyes don't move in their sockets, they can swivel their heads more than 180 degrees to look in any direction.

Plumicorns

The great horned owl gets its name from the tufts of feathers on its head called plumicorns. While these tufts look like ears, its ears are actually tiny openings lower down on the skull, hidden beneath feathers.

Stealth Hearing

A concave arrangement of facial feathers helps direct sound to their ears. Their hearing is so good they can hear a mouse stepping on a twig 75 feet (23 meters) away!

Patterned Feathers

The great horned owls' mottled and striped feathers allow them to blend into the surrounding tree bark.

Whoooo's There?

Squirrels, black bears, elk, ruby-crowned kinglets, and acorn woodpeckers all share this redwood forest with the great horned owl. Can you see all eleven owls hiding in tree hollows and blending into their surroundings?

Polar Bear

Polar bears live on ice-covered waters around the Arctic Circle, inhabiting parts of Canada, Greenland, Norway, Russia, and the United States. The sea ice provides them with access to food (primarily seals) and a place to rest and breed, but melting ice—a result of climate change—means their habitat is shrinking fast.

Big Foot

With paws measuring up to 12 inches (30 centimeters) across, polar bears' giant feet act like snowshoes and distribute their weight on thin ice and deep snow. Their footpads have small bumps called papillae, which stop them from sliding on the slippery ice, and their long curved claws provide extra grip and grabbing power.

Black *and* White

The hairs of a polar bear are colorless and hollow and only appear white because of the way light refracts through the fur—the skin underneath is actually black! This white-looking fur helps a polar bear blend in with its snow and ice environment, allowing it to sneak up on unsuspecting prey.

Marine Mammals

Polar bears are the only bears to be considered marine mammals because they spend so much of their lives on sea ice rather than land. They can run up to 25 miles (40 kilometers) per hour on land in short bursts, swim around 6 miles (10 kilometers) per hour, and hold their breath for more than two minutes. In fact, their Latin name, *Ursus maritimus*, translates to "sea bear"!

A Spotless Coat

After eating, polar bears will often roll in snow or go for a swim to clean their coat. Keeping their fur clean helps protect the insulating properties of their coat and maintain that spotless white they need for camouflage.

Sniffing Out a Meal

Polar bears can smell a seal from more than half a mile (1 kilometer) away or even when their prey is hiding under 3 feet (1 meter) of snow!

Colors of the Arctic

Seals, Arctic terns, kittiwakes, and common eiders all coexist on the Arctic plains, with the threat of polar bears sniffing them out! There are ten polar bears in this landscape—can you see them all?

Leaf and Stick Insects

Leaf and stick insects, also known as phasmids, use their leaf- and twig-shaped bodies to camouflage themselves into surrounding trees. There are around three thousand phasmid species, 150 of which are found in Australia, including the children's stick insect, the spiny leaf insect, and the gargantuan stick insect.

Motion Masquerade

Leaf insects typically sway back and forth when hanging on branches to mimic foliage rustling in the wind and avoid detection by predators.

Leafy Camouflage

The children's stick insect lives on eucalyptus trees and feeds on their leaves. The long yellow strip that runs down the center of its body makes it look almost exactly like a eucalyptus leaf and helps it hide from predators.

Parthenogenesis

Many phasmids are able to reproduce via parthenogenesis. In this process, a female phasmid produces offspring without a male mate, laying eggs that hatch only females.

Gargantuan Giant

Measuring around 20 inches (50 centimeters) long, the gargantuan stick insect is one of the longest insects in the world. These elusive climbers are extremely rare, and their sticklike bodies make them all the more difficult to find amid the forest canopy.

Peanut Butter Defense

The spiny leaf insect is typically found hanging from trees, its body resembling a dried leaf amid the foliage. When threatened, adults produce an odor that smells like peanut butter or toffee to humans, but smells unpleasant to predators.

Stick or Insect?

Kookaburras, koalas, rainbow lorikeets, and yellow-crested black cockatoos all like a good perch. There are ten children's stick insects, five gargantuan stick insects, and two spiny leaf insects among these eucalyptus trees. Can you find them all?

Owl Butterfly

Owl butterflies are primarily found in the rain forests of Central and South America and Mexico. The eye-shaped circles on their wings resemble the eyes of an owl. These eyespots may scare predators away or confuse the predator to aim for the "eye" on the lower part of the wing and not the body, thus giving the butterfly a greater chance of escape.

Hanging Around

Owl butterflies are crepuscular, which means they are most active at sunrise and sunset. During the day they rest on leaves with their wings held tightly together.

A Flashy Side

The markings on one side of owl butterflies' wings resemble tree bark, while the other side has flashes of purplish blue and yellow, which may startle a predator.

Spread Your Wings

Owl butterflies are one of the largest butterflies in Central America, with a wingspan of up to 8 inches (20 centimeters). In fact, their wings are so big that they tend to fly only a few yards at a time before needing a rest!

Life Cycle

1. Egg
Butterfly eggs are very small and are laid on plants by the female. These plants then become food for the hatching caterpillars (also known as larvae).

2. Larva (Caterpillar)
Several days after the eggs are laid, caterpillars emerge and gorge themselves on leaves. As a caterpillar grows, it sheds its skin four or five times.

3. Pupa
When a caterpillar is fully grown, it stops eating, attaches itself to a branch, and forms a pupa (also known as a chrysalis). This cocoon resembles the head of a viper snake, another deterrent for predators! Within the chrysalis the caterpillar changes in a process called metamorphosis. It grows wings, legs, and eyes and transforms into a butterfly.

4. Butterfly
When the butterfly first emerges from the chrysalis, its wings are soft and folded against its body. It pumps blood into the wings to get them working so it can fly and find a mate to start the life cycle again.

Who's Looking at You?

Not all eyes are what they seem! Hiding from the gaze of keel-billed toucans, squirrel monkeys, slender sheartails, and yellow-winged tanagers are seventeen owl butterflies! Don't forget to look for the patterns on both sides of their wings!

African Leopard

The African leopard is found in sub-Saharan Africa, from mountainous forests to grasslands and savannas. They are powerful big cats, closely related to lions, tigers, and jaguars.

Spots

Leopards' spots help them blend into their surroundings—tall grasses and dappled sunlight when on the ground or leaves when climbing in trees. This spotted camouflage helps them get close to their prey before they pounce.

Black Roses

The spots on a leopard's coat are called rosettes because their shape is similar to that of a rose. There are also black leopards (sometimes referred to as black panthers) whose spots are hard to see because of their dark fur, although these types of leopards are more common in Asia.

Spring into Action

Leopards are fast felines and can run up to 36 miles (58 kilometers) per hour. When hunting, they spring into action and can leap 20 feet (6 meters) forward and 10 feet (3 meters) straight up.

Tree Fridge

Leopards are the strongest climbers of all the big cats and will often store carcasses up trees. They are capable of carrying animals heavier than themselves up trees to protect the carcasses from scavengers.

Lone Hunter

Leopards are solitary animals and spend most of their time alone. They are also nocturnal, hunting for prey at night, and spend most of their days resting, camouflaged in trees or hiding in caves.

Leisurely Lying Low

African leopards are most active between sunset and sunrise, when they hunt for prey—giant eland, kudu, springboks, and even giraffes all have to be on the lookout! There are fifteen leopards waiting for the light to fade so they can pounce into action!

Three-Toed Sloth

The three-toed sloth is the world's slowest mammal. In fact, it's so slow that algae grows on its furry coat! The green algae makes the sloth's fur look a little green, which means it can blend in with the trees of the Central and South American rain forests where it lives.

A Leisurely Pace

Sloths move through the forest canopy at a mere 6–8 feet (1.8–2.4 meters) per minute, eating leaves, buds, and fruits. They also have very low metabolic rates, taking them a long time to convert food into energy, and can spend ten to fifteen hours a day sleeping.

Symbiotic Relationship

The algae camouflages the sloth, but what's in it for the algae? The sloth's fur provides the algae with a healthy supply of water because sloth fur is very absorbent. They have a symbiotic relationship, meaning each creature depends on the other for something it needs.

Hanging Out

Sloths are arboreal animals, meaning they spend nearly all their time in trees, gripping branches with the help of their long, powerful claws. They descend to the ground only to find a mate, establish new territory, or poop (which they do only once a week!).

Speedy Swimmers

Sloths' long arms make them surprisingly good swimmers! Swimming helps them travel faster and farther when searching for a mate or looking for new territory.

Slow Food Movement

Sloths conserve movement and metabolize their food slowly—it can take up to a month for a sloth to digest one meal! This means they are rarely hungry and don't need to compete with other animals as often for food.

Slothful Swaying

Three-toed sloths spend most of their time suspended in the treetops among birds like the hyacinth macaw, red-and-green macaw, plum-throated cotinga, and oropendola. Can you spot all twelve sloths in this rain forest?

Mimic Octopus

Mimic octopuses are predominantly found in shallow river mouths and estuaries of the Indo-Pacific, from New Caledonia, the Philippines, Thailand, Indonesia, and Malaysia to as far south as the Great Barrier Reef in Australia.

Amazing Actor

It's estimated that the mimic octopus can imitate around fifteen animals, including sea snakes, stingrays, lionfish, jellyfish, poisonous flatfish, sole, eels, starfish, and coral. It is the only known marine animal able to mimic such a wide variety of ocean life.

The primary purpose of this mimicry is protection from predators (as most of the animals it imitates are poisonous or bad-tasting). However, the mimic octopus can also imitate species such as crabs to get close to prey before pouncing.

Color and Contortion

The mimic octopus can change its skin color and texture using cells equipped with pigment sacs called chromatophores. This ability to blend in with its environment, combined with the ability to contort its body to take on the appearance of other animals, makes it a master impersonator.

Master Impersonator

1. **Jellyfish:** The octopus spreads its arms and lets them gently float in the water to resemble a jellyfish.
2. **Sole:** The octopus pulls its arms in and flattens its body to mimic a sole.
3. **Lionfish:** The octopus spreads out its arms to resemble the lionfish's venomous brown-and-white spines.
4. **Sea Snake:** The octopus pulls six of its arms into a burrow and leaves two out to resemble the venomous sea snake.

Choosing Its Roles

The mimic octopus chooses which animal to impersonate based on which predator is nearby. For example, if bullied by a territorial damselfish, it will mimic a sea snake, a well-known predator of the damselfish.

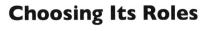

A Variety of Disguises

In the shallows and estuaries of the ocean you might find stingrays, manta rays, great barracuda, sailfin snapper, and orangespine unicornfish . . . but can you find the eight mimic octopuses?

Brown Vine Snake

The brown vine snake is usually found hanging in trees or low shrubs, where, as its name suggests, it is easily mistaken for a vine. It inhabits mostly arid environments, including dry forest edges, thickets, wooded grasslands, brushy hillsides, and densely vegetated canyons. Its habitat ranges from southern Arizona in the United States through Mexico to northern South America and Trinidad and Tobago.

Sticking Around

Remaining motionless, vine snakes disguise themselves as vines or sticks and wait to pounce on unsuspecting prey. They will sometimes flick their bright-colored tongue back and forth to use it as a lure; the motion attracts insects that mistake the tongue for a worm.

Everything Is Just Vine

Very thin and vine-like in appearance, the brown vine snake can grow up to 6 feet (2 meters) long. Its various shades of gray, silver, and copper help it blend in with its surroundings.

Rear-Fanged

The brown vine snake is rear-fanged, or opisthoglyphous, meaning its fangs are found at the back of the upper jaw rather than at the front, like other snake species. It uses venom to kill its prey, but is only mildly venomous and not considered dangerous to humans. Its main prey are lizards, but it will occasionally eat insects, frogs, and birds.

Open Wide!

If in danger, the vine snake will sometimes hold its mouth wide open, exposing the dark lining within to make itself look larger and more threatening.

Defensive Farting

When threatened, the vine snake will sometimes release foul-smelling secretions from the vent on the bottom of its tail.

Stealthy Slithering

Brown vine snakes like to hang very still from trees and branches until unsuspecting prey comes along. In these shrubs you will find bronzed cowbirds, cardinals, eastern meadowlarks, sparrows, frogs, lizards, and twelve snakes!

Gaboon Viper

Gaboon vipers are usually found in rain forests and woodlands of Central, East, and West Africa. They are terrestrial snakes, meaning they stay on the ground and don't climb trees like some other snakes.

Hinged Fangs for Storage

A viper's fangs are attached to the jaw by a hinge, so they can be folded up against the roof of the mouth when not in use. This folding action allows the Gaboon viper to have the longest fangs of any venomous snake in the world! Its fangs can grow up to 2 inches (5 centimeters) in length, and its large venom glands produce the largest quantity of venom of any venomous snake.

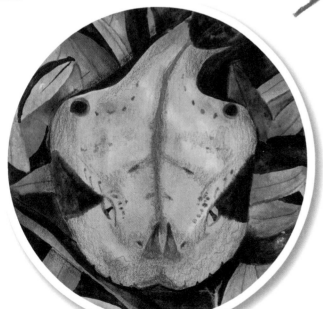

Leaf Head

The Gaboon viper's leaf-shaped head is marked with a dark central vein, much like a fallen leaf. Their bodies are patterned with rectangles and triangles of light yellow, purple, and brown, which help them blend seamlessly with leaves and roots on the forest floor.

Big Snake

Gaboon vipers are the largest vipers in Africa, weighing up to 45 pounds (20 kilograms) and reaching lengths of more than 6 feet (2 meters). Some vipers even have heads nearly 6 inches (15 centimeters) wide! Because of their large bodies, adults can eat prey as large as fully grown rabbits.

Hunting by Ambush

Primarily nocturnal, Gaboon vipers are slow-moving and generally unaggressive snakes. They hunt mostly by ambush, disappearing into the forest floor and waiting for suitable prey to pass within striking distance.

A Predator Underfoot

The Gaboon viper shares its rain forest habitat with many animals—African forest elephants, okapis, and chimpanzees all have to watch where they step! Can you find all eleven vipers on this page?

Ornate Wobbegong

The ornate wobbegong is a species of shark that is mostly found in the Pacific Ocean near eastern Australia. Its patterned markings allow it to hide among plants and reefs, making it the perfect camouflaged predator! Wobbegongs are also referred to as carpet sharks because they are bottom-dwelling sharks that stay close to the ocean floor.

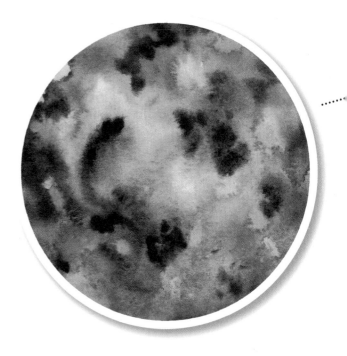

Shaggy Beard

Wobbegongs have whiskers and skin flaps, called barbels, around their nose and mouth that resemble plantlike growths. This bearded fringe acts as both camouflage and bait for the small fish it feeds on.

Watch Your Step!

Ornate wobbegongs usually don't bite humans. However, because they're so well camouflaged, swimmers and divers often fail to see them and sometimes accidentally touch or step on them, making them a little angry!

The Art of Ambush

Wobbegongs patiently wait for prey to come close . . . and then pounce with a quick snap! They swallow small prey whole, or if the prey is too large, they hold it within their jaws (sometimes for days) until it dies. Then they can eat without a fight!

Night Owl

The wobbegong is nocturnal, meaning it's most active at night. During the day it rests out in the open or under rocks and ledges. Although it has poor eyesight, it can use its barbels to sense its environment.

Walk on Water

Wobbegongs can move across the ocean floor using their bottom fins, giving them the appearance of walking. Some have been seen climbing out of the water from one tide pool to another. As long as their gills are wet, they can survive this quick adventure!

Immersive Experience

Ornate wobbegongs use their markings to blend in with the reefs and plants around them. Triggerfish, blue tangs, humphead wrasse, giant trevallies, and groupers all swim around as twelve wobbegongs stealthily stay out of sight!

Orchid Mantis

Found in the rain forests of Southeast Asia, the orchid mantis is one of several species known as flower mantises because of their striking resemblance to flowers. They wait patiently on branches to catch small insects such as crickets, flies, butterflies, and bees.

Aggressive Mimicry

Using a special type of camouflage called aggressive mimicry, the orchid mantis doesn't try to hide to lure its prey, but instead stands out and mimics the look of a flower. Insects are attracted to what they think is a meal, only to be eaten for lunch!

Not an Orchid

Orchid mantises aren't actually trying to imitate a particular orchid. By having colored markings that suggest a "generic" flower, or a close approximation of several different flowers rather than an identical match of a specific species, they are able to lure more types of prey.

A Firm Hold

Mantises have spiky saw-toothed forelegs that help them hold on tight to caught prey.

Deadly Hunter

The mantis climbs up twigs and branches and waits patiently for prey by imitating a flower. It clings to a perch with its two back legs, sways from side to side to look more enticing, and quickly snatches prey with its front legs once in reach.

Changing Colors

By detecting changing light and humidity, the mantis can adapt its color to resemble surrounding flowers within a few days, changing between white, pink, yellow, and purple.

Changing Hues

Birds like the whiskered treeswift, jambu fruit dove, Raffles's malkoha, and scarlet-rumped trogon love an orchid mantis snack! Can you find all thirteen mantises before they do?